Charles Dickens
and his Circle

Lucinda
Hawksley

In memory of my father

Published in Great Britain by National Portrait Gallery Publications,
National Portrait Gallery, St Martin's Place, London WC2H 0HE

For a complete catalogue of current publications please write to the
address above, or visit our website at www.npg.org.uk/publications

First published 2016

ISBN 978 1 85514 596 2

A catalogue record for this book is available from the British Library.

Managing Editor: Christopher Tinker
Copy-editor: Helen Armitage
Design: Smith & Gilmour
Editorial and Production Assistant: Kathleen Bloomfield
Production Manager: Ruth Müller-Wirth
Printed and bound in China

The publisher would like to thank the copyright holders for granting
permission to reproduce works illustrated in this book. Every effort
has been made to contact the holders of copyright material, and
any omissions will be corrected in future editions if the publisher
is notified in writing.

Sold to support the National Portrait Gallery, London

Contents

Charles Dickens
Daniel Maclise, 1839

Dickens and Me

When I was at primary school, my teacher asked if any of us had heard of Charles Dickens. I was amazed she knew his name, because, until that moment, I had only known him as one of my ancestors – he is my great-great-great-grandfather. It was then I realised he was famous outside my family. At school, I studied very little Dickens, which was probably a good thing, so I read some of his novels in my own time, then studied him at university and learnt to love his writing. Several years later, when I began writing my biography of his artist daughter, Katey, I came to know him as a person. Researching Dickens as a father – and he was an indulgent and loving father, compared to most Victorian images of the paterfamilias – was vastly different from studying Dickens the writer. While looking into my own family history for that biography, I came to know the man behind the novels: his good points (of which there were many), his bad points (of which there were also many) and his extraordinary, charismatic personality that sparkles across the decades and the five generations that separate him from me.

Lucinda Hawksley

Boz.

THE MAN BEHIND THE NOVELS

In 1849, the *Oxford English Dictionary* defined 'celebrity' in a new way, as meaning a 'celebrated person, a public character'; the word began to be used when describing Charles Dickens. Yet anyone who had known Dickens as a child must have been astonished to realise that he had evolved from being, in his own words, 'a little labouring hind' to become one of the most famous and adored men in the world.

Charles Dickens is often described as the first 'modern' author, by which it is meant that he went on book and reading tours, and engaged with his public in a manner considered more a twentieth-century phenomenon. Through his sheer force of will he propelled himself out of a rather depressing existence into a sphere of glittering parties and a circle of intelligent, radical, questioning friends who were determined, as was he, to leave the world a better place than when they had come into it. Guests at his parties could expect to meet actors, artists, radical politicians, prison reformers, philanthropists and musicians, as well as writers. Although he has come to be seen as an elderly-looking Victorian with a long, grizzled beard, as a young man he modelled himself on his heroes, the Romantic poets: clean-shaven, long-haired and dressed in the brightest colours that

....
OPPOSITE
Charles Dickens
Samuel Laurence, 1838

early Victorian fashion permitted (as can be seen in Samuel Laurence's portrait on page 6).

Dickens's literary friends included Wilkie Collins, Elizabeth Gaskell, William Makepeace Thackeray and Alfred, Lord Tennyson. He also admired and surrounded himself with artists, including two of his oldest friends, Daniel Maclise and Augustus Egg, the celebrity painters Clarkson Frederick Stanfield, William Powell Frith and John Everett Millais, and many of his illustrators: Hablot Knight Browne (aka 'Phiz'), George Cruikshank, and the father and son Frank and Marcus Stone. He worked tirelessly with fellow social reformers including Angela Burdett-Coutts, Thomas Noon Talfourd and Elizabeth Jesser Reid (the philanthropist and anti-slavery activist, who founded the Ladies' College in Bedford Square, London, where Dickens's daughter Katey later studied art). Although many of Dickens's friends were famous, many were not. Dickens did not court people for their celebrity; he was interested in them because of their beliefs, their actions and their work.

....

When Charles Dickens was born, in Portsmouth, on 7 February 1812, his father, John Dickens, was working as a payroll clerk for the British navy. Charles's mother, Elizabeth Dickens (née Barrow), was a fun-loving, intelligent woman, who intended to teach her children as much as possible before they required expensive schooling. Ironically, despite working in finance, John was incapable of living within his means, a situation not helped by a growing family. The Dickenses spent much of Charles's childhood fleeing landlords they could not afford to pay and borrowing money from friends. The situation worsened when John's job was moved from Kent (where the family had been living for several years) to London, the most expensive place to live in Britain. Shortly after Charles's twelfth birthday, John was arrested for debt and sent to the Marshalsea Debtors' Prison in Southwark, south London.

Charles Dickens's birthplace, 387 Mile End Terrace, Southsea, Portsmouth
Unknown photographer, early twentieth century

Within a short time, Elizabeth and the younger children had joined John, together with their servant girl, inside the prison. Charles's older sister, Frances 'Fanny' Dickens, was at the Royal Academy of Music – a scholarship student whose fees and living expenses were covered – but Charles had been sent out to work. His was a humiliating job for a boy who had dreamed of the kind of gentlemanly future of which young Pip dreams in *Great Expectations*. The job, secured for Charles by a cousin of his mother's, was at Warren's Blacking Factory, on the Strand in central London, where he worked for ten hours a day, six days a week, pasting labels on to bottles.

Fanny Dickens
Samuel Laurence,
c.1836

Dickens remembered it as a smelly, rat-infested place, at which he worked, with deepening humiliation, beside a large window, observed at his labours by all who passed by.

Initially, he lived in Camden Town, north London, in a lodging house run by an unsympathetic acquaintance of his parents. He hated it and was exhausted by walking every day from there to the Strand, and then, sometimes, further south to Southwark for supper with his incarcerated family, before walking

....
Warren's Blacking Factory, London
W. Belson, 1822
Sited on the north bank of the River Thames, close to the site of present-day Charing Cross Station, it was here that Charles Dickens was employed as a child labourer.

back to Camden Town in the dark. It was these long wintry walks – if he went to Southwark, a round trip of almost exactly eight miles – that gave the adult Dickens a keen understanding of the underbelly of London life and the privations of poverty. While he felt himself to be a miserable little boy, he was aware that there were others living in far worse circumstances.

When John Dickens had been arrested, the young Charles feared he would be working in the factory for ever. In reality, John spent just a few months as an imprisoned debtor; his release was secured after the death of Charles's paternal grandmother, who left both her sons (John and William Dickens) a small legacy. John's money went to pay off his creditors, after which he and the family were released from prison, and, astonishingly, John was allowed to return to his job in the payroll office. It took time, however, for Charles to be released from his bondage. Elizabeth was concerned about relying solely on her husband for the family's finances and keen for her son to keep his job – Charles's resentment that his mother should want him to keep on working at such a young age never quite left him, even though she did eventually agree that he should go back to school.

This was not the pleasant school of Dickens's early childhood in Kent but Wellington House Classical and Commercial Academy on Hampstead Road in north London, where the headmaster, a Welshman named William Jones, known by the boys as 'the Chief', was a brutal man. Charles did well there, but, in 1857, remarked that Jones seemed to think it was his business 'to make as much out of us and put as little into us as possible'. His post-blacking-factory schooldays inspired Salem House school and its sadistic headmaster Mr Creakle in *David Copperfield* (the most autobiographical of Dickens's novels).

Although almost no one in Dickens's adult circle knew the truth about his childhood, the spectre of the Marshalsea haunted him to the end of his life. He considered it a shameful time, and the memories and images pervaded his writing. The central character in *Little Dorrit*, written after John Dickens's death, is Amy Dorrit, who is born inside the Marshalsea, where much of the novel's action takes place. In *David Copperfield*, Dickens echoed the advice he recalled his father giving him as they sat together inside John's cell. This advice Dickens puts into the words of Mr Micawber, a jovial debtor and loving husband and father, whose character was based almost entirely on John Dickens: 'Annual income twenty pounds, annual expenditure nineteen [pounds] nineteen [shillings] and

....
Wellington House Academy, Hampstead Road, London
Unknown photographer, n.d.

six [pence], result happiness. Annual income twenty pounds, annual expenditure twenty pounds ought and six, result misery.'

From an early age, Charles felt the responsibility of being the eldest son in a family born to loving but irresponsible parents. It was a responsibility he felt all his life. For his adored older sister – immortalised in *A Christmas Carol* as 'little Fan' – whom he later assisted financially, despite her own success as a musician and music teacher. For his younger sister, Letitia Mary Dickens, to whom he was always close and who he provided for after she was widowed. For one of his younger brothers, Frederick ('Fred') Dickens, whom he tried to stop from going the way of their father, but failed (in *The Old Curiosity Shop*, Charles gave Little Nell's dissolute brother the name Fred).

In 1827, John Dickens was again arrested for debt. On this occasion, the family managed to borrow enough money to keep John out of prison, but the arrest was the catalyst for both Charles and Fanny to leave school and start work properly. Once again, it was his mother's family who found Charles a job, as a clerk in a solicitor's office at the firm of Ellis & Blackmore. Charles distinguished himself on his first day, when he came back from an errand with a black eye after getting into a fight – he retained the wariness of the street child, three years after being forced to live alone. Years later, Edward Blackmore reminisced about Dickens's adolescent working days:

> He was a bright, clever-looking youth ... Several incidents took place in the office of which he must have been a keen observer, as I recognized some of them in his *Pickwick* and *Nickleby*; and I am much mistaken if some of his characters had not their originals in persons I well remember.

············
Alfred Lamert Dickens
Frank Stone, 1849
Alfred died at thirty-eight,
cutting short his promising
career as a pioneering
sanitary engineer. He was
ten years younger than his
famous brother.

Dickens found his job, and the one thereafter, stultifying
and used his spare time to continue his education at libraries and
in learning to write shorthand. Eventually, he made the brave
decision to set himself up as a freelance journalist; in this he was
encouraged by his mother's journalist brother, Thomas Barrow.

With both Charles and John earning enough to support
the family (John had also started working as a freelance
reporter), Charles's youngest brothers, Alfred and Augustus,
benefited from a good education. Alfred became a civil engineer,
who worked on the railways and on sanitation projects. He was a
great inspiration to his author brother, and the two men worked
together on government reports. They talked about ideas for
improving the lives of the poorest people, whose health was
being ruined by the lack of proper sanitation. When the new

General Board of Health was created in the late 1840s, following the passing of the 1848 Public Health Act, Alfred produced an influential – and shocking – report into the lives of the people living in the Canning Town area of London. His report forced the government to examine the problems caused by overcrowding and slum conditions. When Alfred died of pleurisy in 1860, his wife Helen and their five children were left in a financial mess, from which Dickens rescued them. He continued to support them throughout his life, and Helen took over the role of caring for her mother-in-law, Elizabeth Dickens. Alfred's death was a terrible sadness for Charles, as he had been the one brother on whom Charles had been able to rely.

Where Alfred emulated Charles's example, Augustus was more like their brother Fred. In the mid-1850s, Augustus left the promising job that Charles had found for him, attempted a doomed get-rich-quick scheme, abandoned his wife and ran off to America with his pregnant mistress. Augustus had been the adored baby of the family, known by the affectionate nickname of 'Boz'. This was the name that Charles Dickens chose as his pseudonym, when he was commissioned to write a series of 'street sketches' showing daily London life, known today as Charles Dickens's earliest book, *Sketches by Boz*.

....

As a young man Charles Dickens dreamed of being a celebrated actor-manager, a modern-day Shakespeare. Had it not been for a debilitating cold that kept him in bed on the day he was invited to audition for a theatre company, the history of English literature might have been very different.

George Hogarth (1783–1870) and Catherine Dickens (née Hogarth, 1816–79)

One of the people who helped to change Dickens's future was George Hogarth, a lawyer from Edinburgh, who had reinvented himself in London as a newspaper editor. Hogarth was editing the *Morning Chronicle* when he first encountered Dickens's work and commissioned him to write short stories for his newest project, the *Evening Chronicle*. Hogarth also welcomed the young writer to his home, where Dickens fell in love with the eldest daughter, Catherine. Despite the fact that Dickens had little to recommend him, and was hampered by somewhat embarrassing parents, Hogarth could see beyond the superficial and was fascinated by his young protégé. At a time when society deemed it all-important to know about a person's ancestry – who their parents were, how much money they could inherit, what their father did – Dickens should not have been considered a great catch. Hogarth, however, was interested in Dickens's future, not in his past.

Although Catherine Hogarth's remaining letters suggest it was not a case of love at first sight for her, it seems that Dickens fell in love at once with the idea of being part of such a happy, loving family and with their easy middle-class existence. In the Hogarths' pleasant riverside home, there was no taint of prison, or of debt. In February 1835, after Catherine attended Dickens's 23rd birthday party at his bachelor quarters in Furnival's Inn in Holborn, central London, she wrote to her cousin: 'It was a delightful party ... Mr Dickens improves very much on acquaintance, he is very gentlemanly and pleasant.' When Dickens proposed a few weeks later, Catherine accepted.

The couple married on 2 April 1836, at St Luke's Church in Chelsea, and honeymooned in Kent. They set up home at Furnival's Inn and although at the start it was a happy marriage, Charles was disappointed that Catherine did not share his love of energetic walking. Perhaps this was unsurprising, as Catherine became pregnant immediately; their first child, Charles Culliford Boz Dickens, known as Charley, was to be the eldest of ten children: seven boys and three girls. Charles and Catherine were unusual for Victorian parents because they did not believe in physical punishments for their children; many of their friends considered the Dickens children to be spoilt because they were allowed to reason with their parents instead of being 'seen and not heard'. Charles was more enamoured of his children when they were babies and young children than he was when they were adolescents, and he was more indulgent of his daughters than his sons, finding the boys noisy and disturbing when they were all home from school and he was trying to work. A stickler for punctuality and order, he became infuriated if any of the children were late for meals or left their bedrooms in a mess, but his punishment would be a stern note reprimanding them. It seems that the older his sons became, the more disappointed Dickens grew with them; he once wrote to a friend of looking around the dinner table upon the 'lassitude' of his male children. He unfairly blamed this on Catherine, claiming the boys all took after her and had none of his drive or ambition.

....

Catherine Dickens (née Hogarth)
Edwin Roffe, after Daniel Maclise,
c.1848, and (in oval) after John Jabez
Edwin Mayall, n.d. Published 1890

'OUR PATH IS SINGLE AND DISTINCT'

Charley was born while his parents were living at Furnival's Inn, but the wording of Dickens's rental lease forbade children, so his parents began an earnest hunt for a new home. They decided on a pretty town house at 48 Doughty Street in Bloomsbury (now the Charles Dickens Museum). Charles and Catherine Dickens were sociable people who loved parties, and their new home was filled with friends, family and laughter. They stayed at Doughty Street for two years, during which time Dickens worked on *The Pickwick Papers*, *Oliver Twist* (the novel that made him a household name) and *Nicholas Nickleby*, as well as continuing to be a journalist and editor. Mary, known as Mamie, was born in 1838 and their third child, Katey, a year later. Katey was acknowledged by several of her siblings – seemingly without rancour – as their father's 'favourite child' (although when asked about this, she claimed Dickens's favourite child was always David Copperfield).

Katey was the most similar to her father of any of the children, notably because of her fiery temper. After her art studies in London, she became a professional artist and a sought-after portrait painter. In 1860, she married the Pre-Raphaelite artist Charles Allston Collins; after his death in 1873, she married another artist, Carlo Perugini. Mamie never married and once

....
OPPOSITE
Charles Dickens reading to his daughters, Mary ('Mamie')
Dickens and Kate Macready ('Katey') Perugini (née Dickens)
Robert Hindry Mason for Mason and Co., 1865. Published 1880
This family group was photographed in the gardens of the family home, Gad's Hill Place, in Kent. The small inset image is of his eldest son, Charley.

wrote that she was pleased she had never exchanged her father's name for that of another man. The photograph of Mamie and Katey with their father on page 20 was taken in 1865, in the gardens of their family home in Kent. As Dickens sits rather unconventionally on a chair reading to his two adult daughters, Mamie is seated on a low stool, while Katey stands behind her father. It is an apt pose, as Mamie was always subservient to their father, while Katey considered herself his equal and was never afraid to challenge him. Underneath the main photograph is a small image of Charley, as an adult, as if looking on, unable to join the close-knit circle of father and daughters.

With an ever-growing family, the house in Doughty Street began to feel too small, so, in December 1839, the family moved to No. 1 Devonshire Terrace, a grand house opposite Regent's

OPPOSITE
No. 1 Devonshire Terrace,
Marylebone, London
Unknown photographer
Published in the Sketch, 1897
The Dickens family moved
here at the end of 1839,
following the success of
Nicholas Nickleby.

LEFT
'Marley's Ghost' from
A Christmas Carol
John Leech, 1843
This now famous illustration
is of Jacob Marley's ghost,
visiting Ebenezer Scrooge.
Dickens wrote A Christmas
Carol while living at No. 1
Devonshire Terrace.

Park. As always, Dickens threw himself into rapid home
improvements, which included safe, sanitary bathrooms and
indoor 'water closets'. He was more aware than most people
of his time about the dangers of poor hygiene.

Dickens was twenty-seven years old, a household name
and a man who could afford to take on the lease of, as he
described it, 'a house of great promise (and great premium),
"undeniable" situation and excessive splendour'. For the first
time in his life, he had a library. With every step up he took,
he felt he was taking himself and his family ever further away
from the Marshalsea – and getting ever nearer to consolidating
his international success as an author, especially with the
publication of *A Christmas Carol*, *Dombey and Son* and *David
Copperfield*, all written at Devonshire Terrace.

George Cruikshank (1792–1878)

Through his work, Dickens met many of his friends, including George Cruikshank, the illustrator for *Sketches by Boz*, and, later, for *Oliver Twist*. Despite a twenty-year age gap, the two men quickly became friends, sharing radical politics and a belief that the world needed to change, for the better. Born into an artistic family, from the start of his career Cruikshank had been respected for his caricatures and political satire; by the time he met Dickens, he had already earned the title of a 'modern Hogarth'. The two men worked together amicably for more than a decade and often went out drinking, but their relationship changed, after 1847, when Cruikshank joined the Temperance movement, signing a vow of abstinence. Dickens, who knew how to moderate his alcohol

....
OPPOSITE
'Fearful Quarrels and Brutal
Violence are the Natural
Consequences of the Frequent
Use of the Bottle', scene 6 from
'The Bottle' in *Temperance Tales*
George Cruikshank, 1848

....
LEFT
George Cruikshank
London Stereoscopic &
Photographic Company, 1870

intake, disliked both excessive drinking and teetotalism, while
Cruikshank, who had grown up with an alcoholic father, had been
a heavy drinker. Dickens found his friend's new views fanatical and
ridiculous, and was irritated when Cruikshank began preaching
about alcohol. Cruikshank also started to use his artistic skills
to benefit the Temperance movement; most famously with
'The Bottle', a series of eight illustrations, in the manner of
William Hogarth, showing the downward slide of a man and
the destruction of his family, from his first drink through to
poverty, homelessness, violence and insanity. Dickens described
'The Bottle' as 'very powerful', but as his annoyance with the
abstinence movement spilt over into his writing, Cruikshank
began to resent Dickens's attitude. Their friendship started
to suffer and never returned to its former closeness.

....
Augustus Leopold Egg
Thomas Oldham Barlow,
after John Phillip, c.1865

Augustus Leopold Egg (1816–63)

It was also through work that Dickens met the artist Augustus Leopold Egg, who became one of his lifelong friends. Egg had been born into a non-artistic family, the son of a gunsmith, but he enrolled at art school at the age of eighteen and became a member of the artistic group The Clique, which he founded in 1837 with William Powell Frith, Henry Nelson O'Neil, John Phillip and Richard Dadd. Egg is best known for his paintings with a social conscience, notably *Past and Present*, a series of three paintings revealing the treatment of so-called 'fallen women', created by the double standards that were commonplace in misogynistic Victorian Britain.

Egg was a welcome guest to the Dickens home and took an active role in the family's amateur theatricals. These were plays performed every year (sometimes twice) by the Dickens family and a few select friends. It was a great undertaking, with Dickens hiring professional theatrical costumiers, converting the children's schoolroom into a theatre, helping his children learn their roles and inviting a carefully selected audience to his home. As well as acting in many of the plays, Egg also helped design the costumes.

At one stage Egg envisioned turning his friendship with Dickens into an even closer relationship, when he proposed to Georgina Hogarth, Catherine's sister. But she refused his and, indeed, all offers. Having been plagued all his life by chronic asthma, Egg spent many of his final years travelling to warmer climates to ease his breathing. He died during an asthmatic attack in Algiers at the age of forty-six.

Richard Bentley (1794–1871)

As well as being championed by George Hogarth, Dickens was helped in his early career by the publisher Richard Bentley. In 1829, Bentley had begun working with fellow publisher Henry Colburn. They specialised in producing novels of fashionable high life (known as silver-fork fiction) by exciting new authors, including Benjamin Disraeli and the prolific Catherine Gore. Their partnership had proved profitable but stormy, and lasted for only three years, after which the two men entered a legal battle. When Colburn began launching furious attacks against his former business partner in his publication the *Monthly Magazine*, Bentley was prompted into action.

In 1836, the year that Charles Dickens married Catherine Hogarth, Bentley approached Dickens about his idea for a new magazine, of which he wanted Dickens to be editor. The first issue of *Bentley's Miscellany* appeared in January 1837, and Dickens's first editorial included the words:

We do not envy the fame or glory of other monthly publications. Let them have their room. We do not desire to jostle them in their course to fame or profit, even if it was in our power to do so ... Our path is single and distinct. In the first place, we will have nothing to do with politics.

Bentley's Miscellany was the magazine in which Oliver Twist was serialised. However, just as the relationship between Bentley and Colburn had soured, so did that between Dickens and Bentley, following a row, in 1840. The portrait on page 28 was created a few years after he and Dickens ceased working together.

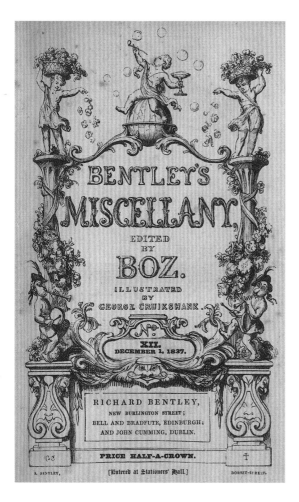

Bentley's Miscellany, no. XII, 1 December 1837
Illustrated by George Cruikshank, 1837
When Dickens first started working on Bentley's Miscellany he was still using the pseudonym 'Boz', but after the serialisation of Oliver Twist, his own name was as famous as his pen name.

John Forster (1812–76)

Another man whom Dickens met in 1836 became his lifelong friend and trusted confidante. He was introduced to John Forster at the house of the novelist William Harrison Ainsworth. The two men were the same age, and there was an instant rapport; many years later, Forster would become Dickens's first biographer.

Forster had arrived in London to study law but decided instead to move into the world of literature. He wrote articles, poems, history books and biographies – of Oliver Goldsmith and Jonathan Swift, among others – and became a well-respected literary critic; he also worked as an editor for publications including the *Daily News* and the *Foreign Quarterly Review*. The watercolour of Forster seen on page 32 was painted in 1840 by his and Dickens's mutual friend, Daniel Maclise; it shows a thoughtful young man, dressed fashionably, as he would have looked at an informal party at Doughty Street or on a night out with Dickens and their friends.

Forster and Dickens shared a love of the theatre, of comedy, of dancing, drinking and dining. At one party, a guest observed them 'exert[ing] themselves till the perspiration was pouring down and they seemed drunk with their efforts! Only think of that excellent Dickens playing the conjuror for one whole hour – the best conjuror I ever saw – and Forster acting as his servant.' Many of Dickens's friends had similar memories of Dickens's infectious childlike delight in parties. He was always willing to entertain both adults and children with his skill at mesmerism, conjuring and magic tricks.

In 1837, Dickens wrote to Forster about his latest project: 'I want you to take some cold lamb and a bit of fish with me, alone.

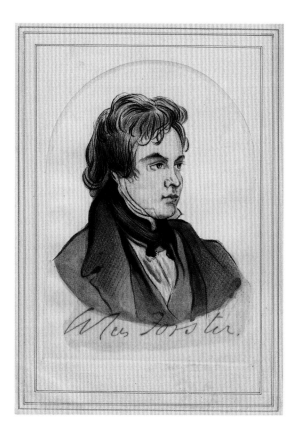

LEFT
John Forster
Daniel Maclise, 1840

OPPOSITE
**'Mr Pickwick addresses
the Club' from
The Pickwick Papers**
Robert Seymour, 1836.
Published 1837

We can walk out both before and afterwards but I must dine at home on account of the Pickwick proofs.' *The Pickwick Papers* was the idea of the publishers Chapman and Hall. They wanted to pair this bright new writer with one of their favourite illustrators, Robert Seymour. It was not a happy partnership. Dickens found Seymour's illustrations stifling and unlike the images he imagined when writing about Mr Pickwick and friends. In April 1836, after another angry meeting with Dickens, and only one published instalment of *The Pickwick Papers*, Seymour, already deeply unhappy, estranged from his wife and children and suffering debilitating bouts of depression, fatally shot himself.

Many years later, when Dickens died, he bequeathed the bulk of his papers and documents to Forster. Six years later, Forster died and bequeathed his collection of books and Dickens's papers to the South Kensington Museum (renamed the Victoria and Albert Museum in 1899).

Hablot Knight Browne (1815–82)

Seymour's replacement was Hablot Knight Browne, best known as 'Phiz'. The illustrator's unusual first name was all he possessed of his real father. He had been brought up as the youngest son of William and Katherine Browne but was actually their grandson. Hablot Knight Browne was, in reality, the son of his pseudo-sister Kate Browne and a dashing French cavalry officer, Nicolas Hablot.

Phiz and Dickens went on research trips, including a journey to Yorkshire, when working on *Nicholas Nickleby*,

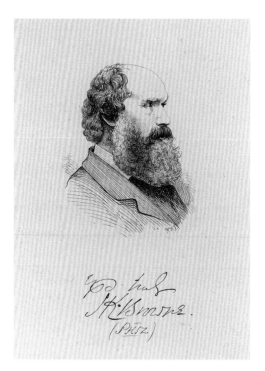

LEFT
Hablot Knight Browne ('Phiz')
Frederick William Pailthorpe, after an unknown artist, late nineteenth century

OPPOSITE
'The internal economy of Dotheboys Hall', from Nicholas Nickleby
Hablot Knight Browne ('Phiz'), 1838–9

to find out if the horrors they had heard about 'Yorkshire schools' – terrible places to which unwanted children were sent, then abused – could be true. They discovered heartbreaking numbers of children's gravestones belonging to former pupils from these schools. Within two years of *Nicholas Nickleby*'s publication, Dickens wrote proudly that every Yorkshire school had been closed down (this was also thanks to the investigative journalists who were inspired by Dickens's novel to visit Yorkshire and find out if what he was writing about existed). By helping Dickens in his research, Phiz was able to recreate the images that Dickens had in mind when writing.

He and Dickens worked together for more than two decades; before Dickens moved to Doughty Street, he and Phiz had been neighbours at Furnival's Inn.

Sir Thomas Noon Talfourd (1795–1854)

Despite his early editorial in *Bentley's Miscellany*, Dickens was seldom far from politics, using his works to laud or lampoon society in general and public figures in particular. He had begun his writing career as a radical journalist and never lost his basic beliefs. He was passionate in his support of those philanthropists and politicians who made a difference to their world. In 1837, when the finished novel of *The Pickwick Papers* was published (after its serialisation was complete), it was dedicated to Sir Thomas Noon Talfourd, a politician, lawyer and writer whom Dickens admired. In this rather grand portrait, by Henry William Pickersgill, Talfourd looks every inch an Establishment figure, but the man who inspired Dickens was an energetic firebrand, who sought – and fought – to bring about legal reform. In 1835, Talfourd had been elected Liberal MP for Reading, and his radical brand of politics agreed with Dickens's own ethics. One of his causes was the plight of women who were kept from seeing their children by estranged husbands. As the law stood, women had no rights, as children were the legal property of the father. Talfourd, inspired by the writings and the personal plight of the campaigner Caroline Norton, was instrumental in the passing of the Custody of Infants Act, 1839. Another cause of which Dickens approved was Talfourd's efforts to change the copyright laws in favour of writers and their heirs. This was a Herculean battle, and one that exhausted Talfourd. He was supported by some of the country's best-loved writers, including William Wordsworth, Thomas Carlyle, Lord Tennyson and Robert Southey as well as Dickens himself, but Talfourd was frustrated at every turn, and the bill was not passed for years. When Dickens was writing *David Copperfield*, his kindly character of Tommy Traddles was based on Talfourd.

Sir Thomas Noon Talfourd
Henry William Pickersgill, n.d.

Clarkson Frederick Stanfield (1793–1867)

In his seminal work *Modern Painters* (1843–60), the art historian John Ruskin would compare Royal Academician Clarkson Frederick Stanfield, a renowned marine and seascape painter, with J.M.W. Turner and describe him as 'the leader of English realists'. When Dickens and Stanfield first met, in 1837, Dickens was in awe of the older man's talent. The two men shared an interest in philanthropy, and Dickens often recruited Stanfield to causes in which he was interested. In 1842, Stanfield, Dickens, Maclise and Forster went on holiday to Cornwall, where they walked for miles. While Dickens and Forster made notes and researched ideas, Maclise and Stanfield painted the scenery. Dickens loved the camaraderie of his male friends, which enabled him to escape the pressures of married life, fatherhood and constant deadlines.

Stanfield went on to contribute illustrations to some of Dickens's Christmas books. He was also invited to illustrate *Pictures from Italy*, the travelogue Dickens wrote after taking his family to live in Italy for a year in 1844–5, but he refused. Stanfield was a devout Catholic and declined to be associated with the book because of its fervent criticism of the Pope. It was surprising that Dickens gave such vent to his anti-papist feelings in *Pictures from Italy*, as his novel *Barnaby Rudge*, published just a few years earlier, had been about the injustices suffered by Catholics in Britain during the 1780 Gordon Riots.

Nonetheless, the friendship was unaffected, and, in May 1855, Stanfield painted an atmospheric backdrop for a theatrical performance of Wilkie Collins's *The Lighthouse* (1855), staged as one of the Dickens family theatricals, with which he, like

Augustus Egg, helped. (The backdrop survives.) At the time, Dickens was writing *Little Dorrit*, which he dedicated to Stanfield. In his mid-thirties when this portrait (below) was painted, he is depicted as a brooding young man.

Clarkson Frederick Stanfield
Attributed to John Simpson, c.1829

John Leech (1817–64)

Another artist friend from these early days of Dickens's career was the illustrator John Leech. Following Robert Seymour's suicide, Leech was one of the illustrators who had applied as a potential replacement. Although he was not chosen for *The Pickwick Papers*, he would illustrate later books, most notably *A Christmas Carol* in 1843. As a young man, John Leech had intended to become a doctor, and it was as a medical student that his great ability for anatomical drawings was noted. He began trying to find work as a book illustrator and soon gave up medicine for art. In 1841, he produced his first cartoon for the satirical magazine *Punch* and became one of its most popular contributors, until his untimely death in his late forties. Leech was also a regular cast member in the Dickens family theatricals. This photograph is a carte-de-visite, dating from two years before he died; he is described on the border of the print as 'John Leech, the caricaturist'.

Leech and his wife Anne (née Eaton) had several children, but only one son and one daughter survived infancy. The young family often travelled with the Dickens family, and in 1849, with a large party of friends, they took a holiday to the newly fashionable Isle of Wight (where Osborne House was being built for Queen Victoria and Prince Albert). One day, when Leech was swimming in the sea, a wave dashed him against a rock, and he was knocked unconscious. The Leech family never forgot how Dickens, who had been learning the art of 'mesmerism', managed to do just that and, in their opinion, save his friend. The local doctor, they felt, was of far lesser importance in Leech's recovery. Ironically, the doctor advised Leech be bled by the application of twenty leeches, which did little to alleviate his condition.

John Leech
McLean, Melhuish & Haes, c.1862

William Charles
Macready
John Jackson, 1821

William Charles Macready (1793–1873)

In 1837, John Forster introduced Dickens to William Charles Macready. Dickens was in awe of the actor, who was fifteen years his senior and whom he had admired on stage. This portrait, by John Jackson, shows Macready as an intense young actor, in the character of Shakespeare's *Henry IV*. It was painted in 1821, when Dickens himself was still a child. The richness of the colours and the extraordinary passion of his stare suggest something of the charismatic personality that drew Dickens, and others, towards him and made Macready such a successful stage personality. By the time he met the young novelist, Macready was famous on both sides of the Atlantic. Perhaps it was their shared experience of difficult childhoods that helped cement their friendship. Like Dickens, Macready had been forced to relinquish his dreams of higher education because his father found himself in financial difficulties. Instead of going to university, Macready joined his father in the often precarious world of theatrical management. Dickens, enamoured of stage life, was captivated by Macready's world and became a willing new friend.

In 1839, after the last instalment of *Nicholas Nickleby* had been printed, the novel was published and dedicated to William Charles Macready. In the same year Dickens asked Macready to be godfather to be his new baby, who was partially named after him: Catherine ('Katey') Elizabeth Macready Dickens. A few months previously, Macready had asked Dickens to stand as godfather to his baby son.

Macready gave Katey Dickens a watch and chain as a christening present, which he proudly noted in his diary was 'very much admired'. He also noted, rather less favourably, how annoying it was to have other babies being christened in the church and how loud was the ensuing dinner party. He was particularly disappointed by some of Dickens's relatives: 'Rather noisy and uproarious – not so much comme il faut as I could have wished.'

In January 1843, Macready's wife, Nina, had had a birthday party, after which Dickens wrote an enthusiastic letter to Macready, who was working in America:

> Good God, how we missed you, talked of you, drank your health, and wondered what you were doing! ... Mrs. Macready looked brilliant, blooming, young, and handsome .... Now you don't like to be told that? Nor do you quite like to hear that Forster and I conjured bravely; that a plum-pudding was produced from an empty saucepan, held over a blazing fire kindled in Stanfield's hat without damage to the lining; that a box of bran was changed into a live guinea-pig, which ran between my godchild's feet, and was the cause of such a shrill uproar and clapping of hands that you might have heard it (and I daresay did) in America.

William Makepeace Thackeray (1811–63)

Another of Dickens's talented friends was the novelist William Makepeace Thackeray. The two men met in the mid-1830s, when Thackeray was trying to decide between a career in writing or art. He applied to illustrate *The Pickwick Papers*, and, like John Leech, he was unsuccessful, but he and Dickens eventually became friendly, and their literary careers often drew parallels – as well as constant rumours of rivalry. Theirs was, at times, a difficult friendship. Thackeray came from a higher social class than Dickens, and their very different backgrounds were a source of simmering contention. Outwardly, they were friendly, but contemporaries who knew them commented on the uneasy atmosphere between the two, especially when both men had a new novel to be promoted.

Like Dickens, William Thackeray began his writing career in journalism and, similarly to Dickens, continued to work as a journalist throughout his life. Dickens set up two magazines: *Household Words* (1850–9) and *All the Year Round* (1859–95, which, after Dickens's death, fell under the editorship of his son Charley). Thackeray was the first editor of the equally popular *Cornhill Magazine*. Both authors used their magazines as a way of publishing not only their own novels in serial form but also work by other writers. The illustration on page 46, entitled 'Authors and Novelists', shows Thackeray, Dickens and a number of their friends – although it was published some years after both men had died. Both are seated in the front row: Thackeray on the left; Dickens on the right. It was just as well that Thackeray was sitting down as, at 6ft 3in tall, he towered over most of his friends. Also in the picture are Edward Bulwer-Lytton, Thomas Carlyle, Anthony Trollope and Wilkie Collins, among others.

LORD BULWER LYTTON
LORD MACAULEY   T . CARLYLE
MAKEPEACE THACKERY   CHARLES   DICKENS
GEO MAC-DONALD   A.J.FROUDE   WILKIE COLLINS   ANTY TROLLOPE
COPYRIGHT

'Authors and Novelists'

Unknown artist. Published by Hughes & Edmonds, 1876

The group includes William Makepeace Thackeray (seated, left),
Wilkie Collins, Thomas Carlyle and Charles Dickens (seated, right)

William Thackeray's home life was very different from that of Dickens. Thackeray was married and had had three daughters with his wife, Isabella, but Isabella suffered a mental breakdown following the death of one of their children, and, as she was considered a danger to herself (having attempted suicide) and her daughters (one of whom she had tried to drown while grief-stricken), the couple lived separately; divorce was not permissible from a spouse who had been declared insane. Anny and Minny Thackeray were close in age to Mamie and Katey Dickens, and the four little girls became firm friends. In adulthood, the Thackeray girls remembered Catherine Dickens with great affection as a shining example of motherhood. They adored their father, who did a superb job in an age when few men embraced single parenthood, but they felt his lack of fashion sense when it came to little girls' dresses and were envious of the Dickens girls' pretty clothes, party shoes and lustrous hair ribbons.

Thackeray and Dickens's difficult, but often affectionate, friendship would reach breaking point following Charles and Catherine's bitter separation in 1858. At this time, Dickens was undergoing a mental crisis that made him unpleasant, not only to his wife but also to many of his long-standing friends and his publishers. Thackeray managed to incur Dickens's wrath, when, in a misguided attempt to straighten out an unfounded rumour being circulated about Dickens, he inadvertently revealed the secret love affair that Dickens was trying to keep hidden. The two men did not speak for five years. In 1863, Katey Dickens (still close friends with Anny Thackeray) effected a reconciliation, at which the two men shook hands and greeted each other warmly. It was fortuitous, if poignant, timing as Thackeray died – suddenly and unexpectedly – just a few months later.

George Henry Lewes (1817–78)

After reading a favourable review of *The Pickwick Papers* by
George Henry Lewes, a critic for leading contemporary journals,
Dickens wanted to meet him, not least because Lewes was from
a theatrical family, which always attracted Dickens's attention.
They met in 1838; this image (below) dates from just two years

George Henry Lewes
Anne Gliddon, 1840

later and shows Lewes as a bohemian young man, holding a large pipe for smoking, standing in front of a bookshelf peopled with the names of his friends and heroes, and resting his elbow on a book by his friend, the poet and critic Leigh Hunt.

Lewes's first memory of Dickens's Doughty Street home was an unfavourable one. He remembered being shown into a room to wait; there he perused the contents of the bookshelves and found them boring, being – as he supposed – books Dickens had been sent to review or that he used for research. Years later, Lewes recalled:

A man's library expresses much of his hidden life. I did not expect to find a bookworm, nor even a student, in the marvellous 'Boz'; but nevertheless this collection of books was a shock. He shortly came in and his sunny presence quickly dispelled all misgivings. He was then, as to the last, a delightful companion, full of sagacity as well as animal spirits; but I came away more impressed with the fulness [sic] of life and energy than with any sense of distinction.

Lewes and Dickens had friends in common, including Lewes's lover, the novelist Mary Ann Evans, better known as George Eliot. Lewes was married when he met her, but his was an open marriage, and his wife, Agnes, was also in an extramarital relationship, with Thornton Leigh Hunt (son of Leigh Hunt). Dickens was a great admirer of Eliot's work. At the beginning, even when everyone else believed her male pseudonym, he was convinced it was the writing of a woman. In later years, he tried to persuade Eliot to let him serialise her work in his magazine, but she resisted.

Daniel Maclise (1806–70)

The most famous portrait of Dickens from these early years of his career was by Daniel Maclise (see page 4). It was painted during the summer of 1839 and shows the author sitting in a red-velvet chair next to his book-laden desk. This was, for most people, the first glimpse of Dickens, as it was reproduced for the frontispiece of *Nicholas Nickleby*; it has become known as 'the Nickleby portrait'.

Maclise was from Cork in Ireland but had emigrated, aged twenty-one, to London, where he had been accepted into the Royal Academy of Arts. He was introduced to Dickens by John Forster. In addition to the Nickleby portrait, he also produced illustrations for Dickens, notably his Christmas books, *The Chimes*, *The Cricket on the Hearth* and *The Battle of Life*. In 1903, Katey Dickens (by now Kate Perugini, married and an artist) was commissioned to write an article for the *Magazine of Art*, 'Charles Dickens as a Lover of Art and Artists'. In it she recalled: 'Maclise ... was very handsome in person, and had a singular fascination of charm and manner, little personal attractions for which my father had invariably an almost boyish enthusiasm, and the charming warmth and geniality of his nature completely won my father's heart.'

Maclise and Dickens's friendship was also immortalised, in a more notorious fashion, during the writing of *Oliver Twist*. In 1837, Maclise had exhibited his portrait *Sir Francis Sykes and his Family* at the Royal Academy's Summer Exhibition. It became the subject of a major scandal, when it was revealed that Sir Francis had discovered Maclise in bed with his wife and was going to name him in a sordid divorce case. After hearing of Maclise's legal woes, Dickens named his villain after his friend's tormentor, safeguarding himself by changing just one letter and making the violent Bill's surname 'Sikes'.

Daniel Maclise
Maull & Polyblank, mid-1860s

Thomas Carlyle (1795–1881) and Jane Baillie Carlyle (1801–86)

In 1840, Dickens was introduced to a man of whom he was already a fan, Thomas Carlyle (who can be seen in the group portrait on page 46). Dickens would later say that he must have read Carlyle's *The French Revolution* (1837) around 500 times, and when he published *A Tale of Two Cities*, in 1859, he cited it as his main inspiration. The two men met for the first time at the house

Jane Baillie Carlyle (née Welsh)
Samuel Laurence, c.1852

of Whig politician Edward Stanley, and Dickens was star-struck by the older man, whose radical politics chimed so well with his own; he had already shared Carlyle's writings on Chartism with his friends. Carlyle, who was somewhat scathing of those who wrote fiction for a living, nonetheless liked Dickens. He recorded his first impressions of him as 'a fine little fellow ... a face of most extreme *mobility* ... [a] shrewd-looking little fellow, who seems to guess pretty well what he is and what others are'.

It was not long after that first meeting that Jane Baillie Carlyle, Thomas's wife, was introduced to the Dickens family. A fascinating and fiery woman, as this portrait suggests, the Carlyle marriage was equally tempestuous. The artist Samuel Laurence was a friend of Charles and Catherine Dickens, as well as of the Carlyles, and fittingly painted Jane in a modern style, in profile, against a background of a rocky landscape. The only brightness in the canvas is the sheen of her skin tone. At first glance she looks stern and unflinching, but a closer look reveals that her nose is tilted slightly upwards as her lips are starting, almost imperceptibly, to smile.

The Dickens children remembered afternoon tea parties at the Carlyles' home in Cheyne Row, Chelsea (then an artistic and bohemian area of London). William Thackeray wrote that the Carlyles lived 'in perfect dignity in a house in Chelsea with a snuffy Scotch maid to open the door and the best company in England ringing at it!'. Katey Dickens had fond recollections of her father and Thomas Carlyle playing enthusiastically at what other adults would have considered children's games; she particularly remembered one called Earth, Air, Fire and Water, in which her father and Carlyle raced around the room throwing a knotted handkerchief at one other and shouting excitedly.

Mark Lemon (1809–70)

Another close friend, and someone much loved by the whole family, was Mark Lemon, the first editor of Punch. He and his wife Helen had two daughters, Alice (known as 'Lally') and Betty, who were great friends with the Dickens girls. Lemon was also a regular participant in the Dickens family theatricals. The children adored him – and were intrigued by the enormity of his paunch. This well-rounded belly – which can be seen to perfection in the caricature opposite – earned him the nickname of 'Uncle Porpoise'. In 1848, Lemon published a children's book, a fairytale named The Enchanted Doll, which he dedicated to the Dickens daughters. The following year, when the Dickens and Leech families were holidaying in Brighton, they implored Lemon to join them, sending him a poem, written by Charles Dickens, which included the lines:

Oh my Lemon round and fat
Oh my bright, my right, my tight 'un
Think a little what you're at –
Don't stay home, but come to Brighton!

The friendship with Lemon – whose daughters were considered such a part of the family that Charles and Catherine Dickens took them on a holiday to Boulogne without their parents – came to an end at the same time as the Dickenses' marriage, in 1858. At this time, when Dickens was at his most depressed, angry, guilt-stricken and unpleasant, he took out his fury on many of his friends, as well as his wife. At the start of the separation, Dickens asked Lemon to take care of Catherine and ensure she received every assistance and proper legal representation; later he accused Lemon of taking Catherine's side. The two men did not speak for six years, although the friendship was renewed in 1864, when they met at the funeral of a mutual friend and were reconciled.

Mark Lemon
Harry Furniss,
1880s or 1890s

CHARLES DICKENS'S

DRAMATIC READINGS

AS READ IN AMERICA.

DOCTOR MARIGOLD.

BOSTON:
LEE & SHEPARD, Publishers.
1876.

BOZ-MANIA: DICKENS IN AMERICA

On 3 January 1842, Charles and Catherine Dickens set sail for North America on board SS *Britannia*, leaving their four children in the care of an able army of family and servants (their fourth child, Walter, had been born in 1841). They sailed out of Liverpool with their maid Anne Brown and, after a turbulent journey beset by seasickness, reached Boston (via Halifax) on 22 January, a couple of weeks before Dickens's thirtieth birthday. Although he had been expecting – and hoping for – adulation, even Dickens was shocked by how much attention and publicity he attracted. In February, he wrote to John Forster, 'I can do nothing that I want to do, go nowhere where I want to go, and see nothing that I want to see. If I turn into the street, I am followed by a multitude.' Not all Americans were enchanted by Dickens, however; many contemporary reports show that observers found him a little too loud, too brash, too vulgar. For some, he was the epitome of glamour; for others, he was not the perfect English gentleman they had expected – mostly because he made comments that offended puritanical sensibilities, such as describing a woman as 'kissable', combing his unruly hair in public and dressing like a dandy.

....
OPPOSITE
Poster advertising 'Charles Dickens's Dramatic Readings as read in America'
Published by Lee & Shepherd of Boston, MA, 1876

Mindful of Thomas Noon Talfourd's work on copyright law, Dickens arrived in America armed with a petition calling for a proper legal position for international copyright. Dickens had heard stories of huge crowds thronging to greet the ships that brought the latest copies of his works to Boston and New York's harbours, and he received regular letters from American fans who had read everything he had written; yet he didn't receive a penny of the profits because there was no reciprocal copyright law between Britain and America. His works would be bought in London, shipped across the Atlantic and then hastily transcribed before being sold on to make a fat profit for the publishers and printers. Neither British nor American authors were happy about this: the British, because they didn't get paid for their work; the Americans, because the pirated works were sold much more cheaply than their own novels could be. Writers on both sides of the Atlantic were longing for a change in the law; publishers and readers were not. Despite Dickens's best efforts, international-copyright law would not change in his lifetime. He was disheartened by the lassitude of American authors in helping him in this cause, believing they were all of the same opinion as he but too scared to say anything.

Shortly after arriving in Boston, Dickens hired a travelling secretary, George Washington Putnam, whom he affectionately nicknamed 'Hamlet'. The two men were the same age, and, in an America where slavery was still rife, Putnam's strong Abolitionist views were welcome to Dickens. Putnam was so liked by Charles and Catherine that they soon doubled his monthly salary. Many years later, Putnam published his memoirs, *Four Months with Charles Dickens* (1870), including a story of their time in St Louis:

One day a well-known literary gentleman called and was cordially received by Mr. Dickens. After conversing for some time he began to speak of the condition of society in America, and at last in a most bland and conciliating manner asked: 'Mr. Dickens, how do you like our domestic institution, sir?' 'Like what, sir?' said Mr. Dickens, rousing up and looking sharply at his visitor. 'Our domestic institution, sir, slavery!' said the gentleman. Dickens's eyes blazed as he answered promptly, 'Not at all, sir! I don't like it at all, sir!' 'Ah!' said his visitor, considerably abashed by the prompt and manly answer he had received, 'you probably have not seen it in its *true* character, and are prejudiced against it.' 'Yes, sir!' was the answer, 'I have seen it, sir! all I ever wish to see of it, and I detest it, sir!'

The gentleman looked mortified, abashed, and offended, and, taking his hat, bade Mr. Dickens 'Good morning' which greeting was returned with promptness, and he left the room. Mr. Dickens then, in a towering passion, turned to me. 'Damn their impudence, Mr. P.! If they will not thrust their accursed "domestic institution" in my face, I will not attack it, for I did not come here for that purpose. But to tell me that a man is better off as a slave than as a freeman is an insult, and I will not endure it from any one!'

Henry Wadsworth Longfellow (1807–82)

Of the many 'well-known literary gentlemen' to whom Dickens was introduced, several stood out in his memory. The poet Henry Wadsworth Longfellow had been a fan of Dickens before most people in America had even heard of him. In 1836, when travelling in Europe, Longfellow had discovered *The Pickwick Papers*. After returning home, he introduced Dickens's work to his friends, with whom he formed a Pickwickian-style club, known as The Five of Clubs. By the time Dickens arrived in Boston, Longfellow was Professor of Modern Languages at Harvard and had published two volumes of poetry. When rumours started to reach Longfellow's ears, in 1841, that Dickens was planning a trip to America, he was determined to meet his hero. He was one of the many Boston luminaries invited to attend the Dickens Banquet taking place a few days before the author's arrival – an indication of the so-called 'Boz-mania' that had gripped the city. When he and several other Harvard professors were invited to meet Dickens at his hotel, Longfellow was thrilled. Dickens wrote to Forster, 'The Professors at the Cambridge university … are noble fellows.' Longfellow's letter to his father was rapturous: 'Dickens has arrived. He is a glorious fellow.'

The following day, Longfellow took Dickens on a long walk all through the city; they walked and talked for, as Longfellow later estimated, about ten miles. It was the start of a friendship that would endure to the ends of their lives. After Dickens returned to England, he and Longfellow remained in regular correspondence, and before the year's end Longfellow visited the Dickens family in London. Longfellow stayed for a fortnight, and, after he had left, Dickens wrote to him with great fondness

....
Henry Wadsworth Longfellow
London Stereoscopic & Photographic
Company, 1850s

of a game his children had made up in Longfellow's memory.
Longfellow stayed with Dickens again, in the 1850s and 1860s;
this photograph (above) was taken at a London studio during
his 1850s visit.

Washington Irving (1783–1859)

While planning his trip to America, Dickens had been looking forward to meeting one of his heroes, Washington Irving. The author, whose works included 'The Legend of Sleepy Hollow' (1820), had found fame in both America and Britain, and, before he left England, Dickens had been thrilled to receive a complimentary letter from Irving about *The Old Curiosity Shop*. The two men began a regular correspondence, and when the Dickens entourage travelled from Boston to New York City one of the first people to arrive at their hotel was Irving. The following week, Irving presided over a banquet held in Dickens's honour. In Irving, Dickens found an ally in his desire to create an international-copyright law – but was frustrated by Irving's, in common with his fellow authors', inability to challenge the status quo. In an outraged letter to John Forster he complained:

The notion that I, a man alone by himself, in America, should venture to suggest to the Americans that there was one point on which they were neither just to their own countrymen, nor to us, actually struck the boldest dumb! Washington Irving, Prescott, Hoffman, Bryant, Halleck, Dana, Washington Allston – every man who writes in this country is devoted to the questions, and not one of them dares to raise his voice and complain of the atrocious state of the law…. It is nothing that I gave a claim to speak and be heard. The wonder is that a breathing man can be found with temerity enough to suggest to the Americans the possibility of their having done wrong. I wish you could have seen the faces that I saw … I wish you could have heard how I gave it out. My blood so boiled as I thought of the monstrous injustice that I felt as if I were twelve feet high.

Despite this, Irving and Dickens remained on good terms while Dickens was in America, though the friendship suffered after he left. Irving was angered by the portrayal of his country in Dickens's travelogue *American Notes*, despite Dickens referring to Irving in the book as 'my dear friend'.

Washington Irving
William Brockedon, 1824

Edgar Allan Poe (1809–49)

Another American writer who, like Longfellow, had been keen to make Dickens's acquaintance was Edgar Allan Poe. The two men met in Philadelphia, after Poe wrote to Dickens requesting a meeting. Poe claimed afterwards that he took much of his inspiration from Dickens. He was intrigued by Grip, the talking raven in *Barnaby Rudge*, and excited to discover that Dickens himself had a pet raven named Grip. This prompted one of Poe's most famous works, 'The Raven' (1845).

Before Dickens's visit to Philadelphia, Poe had written favourable reviews of Dickens's work, and, in gratitude, Dickens hoped to find Poe a British publisher. On 27 November 1842, Dickens wrote to Poe expressing regret that he had been unable, as yet, to do so, but adding that, due to the current state of the publishing world, 'the only consolation I can give you is that I do not believe any collection of detached pieces by an unknown writer, even though he were an Englishman, would be at all likely to find a publisher in this metropolis just now'. Their friendship came to an abrupt end when Poe became convinced that an article about American poetry, in which he was not treated positively, was by Dickens. It was actually by John Forster, but Dickens was unable to convince Poe it was not by him; a dejected and saddened Poe ended their correspondence. Poe died a few years later, aged forty, in what remain mysterious circumstances. This wistful photograph (opposite) was taken a year before he died.

OPPOSITE
Edgar Allan Poe
Samuel W. Hartshorn, 1848

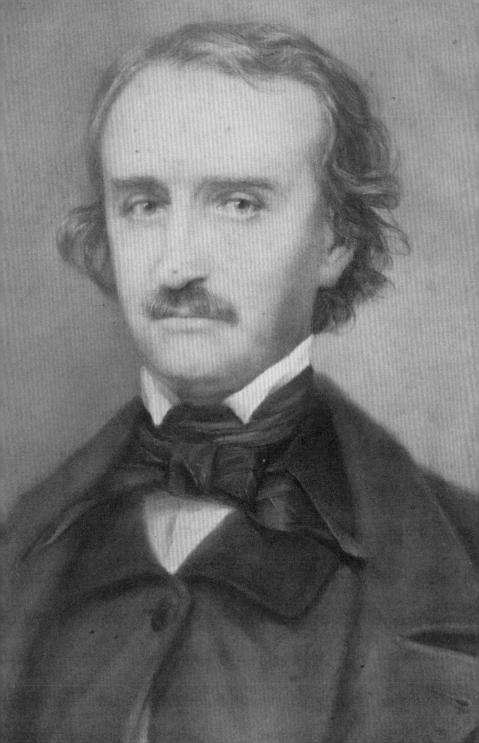

After his return to London in the summer of 1842, Dickens started work on *American Notes*; he also incorporated his less flattering impressions of America into *Martin Chuzzlewit*. Neither book was popular in the country that had shown Dickens so much hospitality. It took a quarter of a century, and a civil war, before Dickens was ready to return to America – and before America was ready to receive him again.

When Charles Dickens arrived back in Boston in the winter of 1867–8, he looked a shadow of the impudent Boz by whom Americans had been alternately charmed and appalled in 1842. He had become a worldwide celebrity, his hair was coarse and grey, he had an unkempt beard – and he was no longer with his wife. The whole world knew that the pretty, adoring Catherine Dickens, who had travelled through North America and Canada with him as a sweet, young bride, was banished from the family home. Despite all this, Dickens was adored even more than before – although this time it was a more mature adoration. This photograph (opposite) was taken at a fashionable New York City studio at the end of 1867.

OPPOSITE
Charles Dickens in New York
George Gardner Rockwood, 1867

James T. Fields (1817–81)

The most influential person waiting to greet Dickens on this second trip to America was the publisher James T. Fields, who had been in his early twenties when Dickens first visited America. Fields was among the throng of admirers who waited to see the celebrated Boz alight from the *Britannia* and then arrive at his hotel. Many years later, Fields published a book entitled *In and Out of Doors with Charles Dickens* (1876); in it, he recalls his first sight of Dickens:

James T. Fields
Julia Margaret Cameron, 1869

He ran, or rather flew, up the steps of the hotel and sprang into the hall. He seemed on fire with curiosity, and alive as I never saw mortal before. From top to toe every fibre of his body was unrestrained and alert. What vigor, what keenness, what freshness of spirit, possessed him! He seemed like the Emperor of Cheerfulness on a cruise of pleasure, determined to conquer a realm or two of fun every hour of his overflowing existence.

Fields, who was already working as a publisher in the early 1840s, determined to work with Dickens. He travelled to England and wrote to the author asking if they could meet. He wanted them to work together, and he offered Dickens a proper American publishing deal, in which Fields would be his official publisher and Dickens would receive royalties from his work. Fields could not prevent other publishing houses from continuing to pirate Dickens's work, but he could publish his own official versions. The two men began a firm friendship that lasted until Dickens's death; James T. Fields's wife, Annie, also became one of Dickens's regular correspondents. This arresting photograph of Fields (opposite) was taken in May 1869, during his visit to England, by the Pre-Raphaelite photographer Julia Margaret Cameron.

············
OVERLEAF
Spectators buying tickets for a Charles Dickens reading at Steinway Hall, 71 East 14th Street, New York City
Illustration from *Harper's Weekly*, vol. 11, no. 574, 28 December 1867

INFLUENTIAL WOMEN

Dickens is often criticised for the way in which he portrayed women in his fiction, usually making them weak and foolish or figures of fun. This is surprising because he was friends with – and related to – so many indomitable, independent, strong-minded women. He grew up with a mother who (unusually, for a woman born in the eighteenth century) had received an education that was sufficiently comprehensive for her to teach her own children rudimentary classics, including Latin. In his early years he was overshadowed by an older sister destined for a professional career in music from a very young age. His female friends included intelligent and capable authors, philanthropists, campaigners and educators.

Perhaps Dickens was portraying in his novels an idealised, contemporary woman – biddable, compliant and domestic (who, to modern readers, appears weak and annoying); perhaps he was writing about the kind of woman he thought his audience wanted to read about. Ironically, he abandoned the woman who seemed to be the epitome of his perfect fictional wives for an actress close in age to his younger daughter. Whatever his reasons for creating such unrealistic female characters, the reality of the women in Dickens's life was very different from his domesticated and compliant heroines.

....
OPPOSITE
Georgina Hogarth and Mamie Dickens
George Herbert Watkins, 1860s

Georgina Hogarth (1827–1917)

Charles and Catherine Dickens returned from America in 1842 with a promise to their children that on all future long trips they would go too. During Charles and Catherine's absence, among the family and servants who cared for the children were Uncle Fred Dickens (Charles's younger brother, Frederick), who was living with them as their guardian, and Catherine's fifteen-year-old sister Georgina Hogarth. Georgina, or 'Aunty Georgy' as she was known by the children, had visited every day she could and became a great favourite; so much so that on their return Charles and Catherine asked her to move in with them.

At this time, it was common for unmarried women to live with their older married sisters. In an age when unmarried women and girls needed to be chaperoned, it was hoped that having a married sister, as opposed to a mother or aunt, as a chaperone would be not only more enjoyable but also more likely to lead to introductions to eligible bachelor friends of her brother-in-law. Georgina, however, steadfastly resisted any such interest.

Georgina soon made herself indispensable within the family – and it took only a few years before Catherine Dickens started to realise that having a slim, enthusiastic, eager-to-please younger sister in the house wasn't necessarily a good idea for a marriage that had started to lose its lustre. Catherine seemed to be perpetually pregnant, or nursing a new baby. Within fifteen years she gave birth to ten children and had at least two miscarriages (as recorded in surviving letters, though Catherine might have suffered others – miscarriage was seldom discussed in nineteenth-century Britain). It is difficult to know why there were such problems in the sisters' relationship, but while

Catherine became less happy and increasingly less capable of coping with such a large number of children, Georgina seemed tireless and always able. She adored her brother-in-law and took his side instead of her sister's in any dispute. After Charles and Catherine separated, Georgina remained living with Charles, looking after the children and serving as his housekeeper, for which she was shunned by her parents and siblings. The photograph on page 72 depicts Georgina and Mamie Dickens holding each other close and reading together; it was taken in the 1860s, after Catherine had left the family home and Georgina had taken over as 'second mother' to the children. In his will, Charles described Georgina as his 'best and truest friend'; as she survived him by several decades, after his death, Georgina was perceived as the authority for information about him. She also outlived most of her nieces and nephews, dying in 1917 at the age of ninety.

Angela Burdett-Coutts (1814–1906)

One of the most influential women in Dickens's circle was the banking heiress Angela Burdett-Coutts. She met Dickens for the first time in the early 1830s and became godmother to Charley (proving a dedicated one: she funded Charley's Eton education). Dickens dedicated *Martin Chuzzlewit* to her. Angela Burdett had never expected to become the most wealthy heiress in England, but following the death of her grandfather, Thomas Coutts, she was discovered to be the principal beneficiary in his will. It was then that she added his name to her own. She was a remarkably principled heiress, using her money to benefit many charitable causes; she began working regularly with Dickens after discovering they shared an ideology. They became good friends, and it was a fruitful partnership, with Dickens tirelessly researching the worthy causes about which he had heard – including the Ragged Schools movement, prison reform and the twin horrors of homelessness and the workhouse – and Burdett-Coutts providing the financial backing.

In 1847, Dickens and Burdett-Coutts set up their most famous joint venture: Urania Cottage in Shepherd's Bush (then a rapidly growing suburb in west London). This was intended as a rehabilitation home for so-called 'fallen women'; a category that could cover all manner of social ills in a Britain in which women were still the legal property of men. Many of the women with whom Dickens and Burdett-Coutts chose to work had been forced to keep themselves and their children alive by thieving

or working as prostitutes; as a result several had been sent to prison. Dickens was friends with many prison governors and often worked with them to help women who were about to be released. He was passionate about the need for rehabilitation and kindness, convinced that most women who ended up in London's prisons were not criminals but simply desperate, having been failed by an uncaring and harsh society. In a letter sent to Burdett-Coutts in 1846, when the idea was starting to come to fruition, Dickens outlined his thoughts as to what the women who were accepted into Urania Cottage should be told:

> [She] has come there for *useful* repentance and reform, and because her past way of life has been dreadful in its nature and consequences, and full of affliction, misery, and despair to *herself*. Never mind Society while she is at that pass. Society has used her ill and turned away from her, and she cannot be expected to take much heed of its rights or wrongs. It is destructive to *herself*, and there is no hope in it, or in her, as long as she pursues it.

The watercolour portrait of Angela Burdett-Coutts on page 77 was painted *c.*1847, at the time when she and Dickens were setting up Urania Cottage. It shows her not as a privileged woman seated contentedly amid her trappings of wealth but as someone deep in thought. She has been reading a book, now closed on the chair, and is depicted as a woman too busy with her ideas to sit still and pose for an artist.

The idea of Urania Cottage was a philanthropic one; it was a moderate success, although many of the residents did not take

Angela Burdett-Coutts
Francis Henry Hart for
Elliott & Fry, 1882

to the strictures that living like a 'gentlewoman' imposed on them.
Of the numerous letters written by Dickens during the decade
in which he and Burdett-Coutts collaborated on Urania Cottage,
it is their perceived failures that make for the best reading. Take
Sesina Bollard: 'the most deceitful little minx in this town ... she
would corrupt a Nunnery in a fortnight!' Urania Cottage and its
founders' friendship were victims of the Dickenses' marriage
breakdown, as Burdett-Coutts found it difficult to forgive her
former friend for his treatment of his wife.

Elizabeth Gaskell (1810–65)

Another female friend whose work Dickens admired, and whose religious convictions he shared, was the writer Elizabeth Gaskell. Both Gaskell's father and her husband were Unitarian ministers. Unitarianism was the religion that had so intrigued Dickens during his first visit to America that he had converted to it upon his return, feeling that the Unitarians 'would do something for human improvement if they could; and practice charity and toleration'. As his novels suggest, he was wary of formalised religion, despising how 'Sunday Christians' showed up in their finery and pretended to be observant and God-fearing, yet did nothing to alleviate the poverty they passed on the streets every day.

It was shortly after his conversion to Unitarianism that Dickens wrote the story for which he remains best known, and it was inspired by Elizabeth Gaskell's home town of Manchester. In 1843, some years before he met Gaskell, Dickens had been invited to the city to help raise funds for a new educational charity. The poverty he saw there had shocked him and inspired *A Christmas Carol*. The following year, Friedrich Engels would publish *The Condition of the Working Class in England*, in which he described 'the workers' dwellings of Manchester ... [as] dirty, miserable and wholly lacking in comforts ... [where] only inhuman, degraded and unhealthy creatures would feel at home'.

In 1848, Elizabeth Gaskell had published, anonymously, *Mary Barton*. When Dickens read the novel he knew that in Gaskell he had found a kindred spirit. He wrote to her in 1850 begging her to let him serialise her work, saying 'there is no living English writer whose aid I would desire to enlist in preference to the authoress of *Mary Barton* (a book that most profoundly affected

and impressed me).' Dickens was invited to the Gaskells' home whenever he was in Manchester. Here he, Elizabeth and William, Gaskell's husband, would talk for hours about how to alleviate society's ills. When he launched his magazine *All the Year Round*, Dickens continued to publish Gaskell's works and to champion her writing. He also guided her and was a sympathetic editor. It is largely due to Dickens's interest in and promotion of her work that Gaskell became famous as a novelist. She refused to be cowed by what the public expected of the wife of a church minister, writing about subjects deemed unsuitable for a female novelist, such as illegitimacy and prostitution in *Ruth* (1853). Gaskell used her friendship with Dickens to promote worthy causes of her own, asking him to help people she was unable to assist herself.

Anne Thackeray Ritchie (1837–1919)

Another female writer who was part of Dickens's circle was Anne Thackeray Ritchie (known as 'Anny'), daughter of William Thackeray and a regular visitor to the Dickens home from childhood. Anny, who was considered by all to be a confirmed spinster, became a successful novelist and, at the age of thirty-nine, shocked London society with news of her engagement. Not only was a woman of almost forty deemed too old for a first marriage but her fiancé was also seventeen years her junior – and her godson. Anny married Richmond Ritchie in August 1877 and confounded Victorian sensibilities by giving birth to a healthy daughter just before her forty-first birthday; a healthy son was born the following year. All the while she continued to write and to make money from her writing. She did everything a Victorian woman was not expected to do – although she was not liberated enough to leave her husband for his frequent infidelities. Ironically, having married someone almost two decades younger than she was, Anny was left a widow in 1912. She and Dickens's daughter Katey remained firm friends until the end of their long lives.

············
OPPOSITE
Anne Thackeray Ritchie
Julia Margaret Cameron, 1870

No. I.   MARCH.   Price 1s.

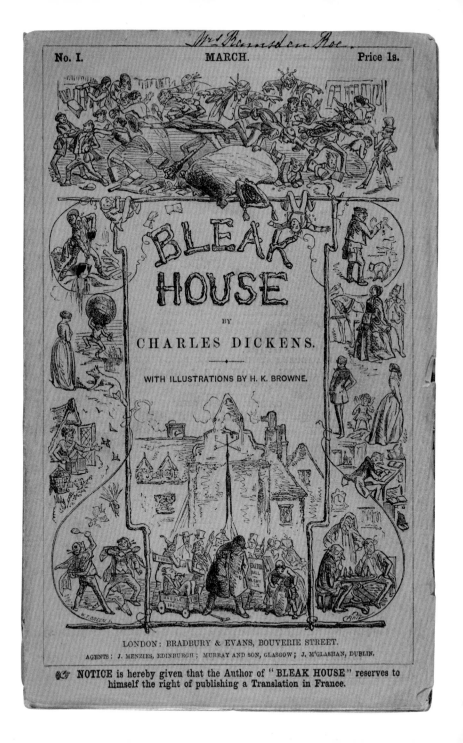

BLEAK HOUSE

BY

CHARLES DICKENS.

WITH ILLUSTRATIONS BY H. K. BROWNE.

LONDON: BRADBURY & EVANS, BOUVERIE STREET.

AGENTS: J. MENZIES, EDINBURGH; MURRAY AND SON, GLASGOW; J. M'GLASHAN, DUBLIN.

FROM BLEAK HOUSE
TO GAD'S HILL

In 1851, the Dickens family moved from Devonshire
Terrace to an even grander home, Tavistock House, in London's
Bloomsbury. The house became Dickens's new project, and for
months before the family moved in he was constantly writing
letters about the improvements needed, the state of the drains,
a rat that had been spied in the kitchen – but mostly about the
problem of finding reliable builders. Henry Austin, the architect
husband of his sister Letitia, oversaw the work, while Dickens
and his wife found themselves to be of little use. In an amusing
letter, he wrote that on one occasion, having gone to the house
in an attempt to hurry the workmen along, Catherine had ended
up being 'all over paint'.

The first novel that Dickens worked on at Tavistock House
was the epic *Bleak House*, which was serialised over two years
and saw Dickens create a new fictional force, that of the literary
detective, in the guise of Inspector Bucket (based on his friend
Detective Inspector Charles Frederick Field of the Metropolitan
Police's newly formed Detective Department).

....
OPPOSITE
**The cover of Bleak House in its original
serialised edition, no. I, March 1852**
Illustrated by Hablot Knight Browne
('Phiz'), 1852

The Stone Family

Among the Dickenses' neighbours at Tavistock House were the artist Frank Stone (1800–59) and his family. Dickens and Stone had met at the Shakespeare Society in the 1830s. The two men shared a love of walking and often went on long hikes together, usually in company with Mark Lemon, John Leech and others. Stone illustrated *The Haunted Man* and later editions of *Martin Chuzzlewit* and *Nicholas Nickleby*; he also took part in the family theatricals. In addition, he was a successful portrait painter, and his many pictures of the Dickens family include, most notably, one of Catherine Dickens. This witty self-portrait (opposite) shows him as an attractive young man, so absorbed in his art that his hat and gloves lie discarded at his feet as he gazes ahead, focused on capturing his image from a mirror.

The Dickens and Stone children were friends. Charles Dickens was particularly fond of Marcus Stone (1840–1921), Frank's son and another budding artist. Marcus was slightly younger than Katey Dickens, and the two often painted together. When Frank Stone died suddenly of an aneurism in 1859, Marcus was only nineteen. Dickens immediately made him welcome within his family and sought out work for him, recommending Marcus to publishing friends and commissioning from him illustrations for new editions of his earlier novels. Marcus would illustrate *Great Expectations* and *Our Mutual Friend*.

It was partly thanks to Dickens's championing of his work that Marcus Stone went on to attain artistic fame and wealth.

....
OPPOSITE
Frank Stone
Self-portrait, 1824

Tavistock House, Bloomsbury, London
Unknown artist, n.d.
Dickens leased this house from his friend
Frank Stone from the autumn of 1851. The
Dickens family moved there a few months
after the death of baby Dora Dickens.

He cultivated the role of 'gentleman–artist', something that became fashionable in the latter half of the nineteenth century, when artists were no longer expected to be bohemian, existing on the fringes, but instead leaders of fashionable society. At the age of eighteen, Marcus had exhibited at the Royal Academy of Arts in London for the first time; he continued to do so, and in 1886 he was elected a Royal Academician. He claimed, however, never to have been satisfied with any of his paintings, writing towards the end of his life: 'At no time have I brought the production of a picture to a conclusion without a keen sense of failure. To exhibit a picture is like publishing evidence of incapacity.' Despite this seeming lack of self-confidence, financially he did well enough to commission the architect Richard Norman Shaw to build him a beautiful home, complete with studio, on Melbury Road, alongside London's Holland Park. This area had become an artistic enclave, and Stone's neighbours included Frederic, Lord Leighton, and G.F. Watts.

Wilkie Collins (1824–89)

Augustus Egg introduced Dickens to the fellow author and *bon vivant* Wilkie Collins around the time the Dickens family moved into Tavistock House. The earliest-surviving letter between them (dated March 1851), sent by Dickens to Collins, concerned the play Dickens was about to stage, which required an extra male actor – for which Collins had been recommended. Within a short time, Collins had been welcomed into Dickens's circle and began taking part in the family theatricals. He was twelve years younger than Dickens and initially in awe of him. Just how famous Dickens was by this date is shown by an incident from the early 1850s, when the Dickens family were spending a summer in Boulogne at the same time as the British royal family. One morning, out on one of his customary walks, Dickens encountered Prince Albert walking with Napoleon III. Queen Victoria's husband raised his hat to the novelist.

The portrait of Wilkie Collins on page 91 was painted in 1850, just before he met Dickens, and is by his family friend John Everett Millais. It captures Collins's unusual looks: his large, domed forehead and deep-set eyes. The two novelists had much in common and became confidantes and travelling companions. John Forster (famously jealous of Collins's closeness to Dickens) wrote, in his 1872–4 biography of Dickens, 'Wilkie Collins became, for all the rest of the life of Dickens, one of his dearest and most valued friends.' In the mid-1850s, the two men embarked on a series of collaborative articles for *Household Words* that would later be turned into a book: *The Lazy Tour of Two Idle Apprentices*. They gave themselves pseudonyms for the articles, which they wrote while travelling around Britain: Collins was Thomas Idle and Dickens was Francis Goodchild. They also collaborated on the mystery story *No Thoroughfare* (1867) and the play *The Frozen Deep* (1857). Collins regularly joined the Dickens family on holidays and was a frequent contributor to Dickens's magazines.

As the Dickenses' marriage fell apart in the 1850s, daughter Katey sought a way to escape without risking her relationship with her father. For a woman of her time, there was only one serious recourse: marriage. When Wilkie Collins's younger brother, Charles Allston Collins, known as Charlie, proposed, Katey accepted. Wilkie Collins was thrilled that his brother would become his friend's son-in-law, but Dickens was less than enchanted with the prospect. The marriage was not a success and remained unconsummated; it seems likely Charlie was homosexual – at a time when British men dared not admit such feelings without risking ostracism, disgrace and prison.

Despite his growing irritation with Charlie Collins, Dickens helped the younger man generously in his career. Charlie had originally been an artist, but decided to become a writer after marrying Katey, and although he was not naturally gifted, Dickens gave him regular work on *All the Year Round*, commissioning him as a columnist. He also tried to give him illustration work: Charlie was the initial illustrator for what turned out to be Dickens's last – and unfinished – novel, *The Mystery of Edwin Drood*. Nonetheless, Dickens found it difficult to conceal his disappointment in his son-in-law, which led to tension in his friendship with Wilkie Collins.

John Everett Millais (1829–96)

Despite his subsequent generosity towards his son-in-law, an article by Dickens, written some ten years before Charlie and Katey's wedding, had – almost unwittingly – blighted Charlie Collins's life. On 12 June 1850, Dickens published 'Old Lamps for New Ones' in *Household Words*, in which he launched a scathing attack on a new art movement: the Pre-Raphaelite Brotherhood. Although Charlie was not one of the Brothers, he was closely associated with them, and it was the work of his best friend, John Everett Millais, that came in for the most acerbic of Dickens's comments, in particular *Christ in the House of his Parents*.

Sir John Everett Millais, 1st Bt
George Herbert Watkins, 1857

In the foreground of that carpenter's shop is a hideous, wry-necked, blubbering, red-headed boy in a bedgown; who appears to have received a poke in the hand, from the stick of another boy with whom he has been playing in an adjacent gutter, and to be holding it up for the contemplation of a kneeling woman, so horrible in her ugliness, that (supposing it were possible for any human creature to exist for a moment with that dislocated throat) she would stand out from the rest of the company as a Monster in the vilest cabaret in France, or the lowest gin-shop in England.

The boy was Jesus; the kneeling woman, the Virgin Mary.

For a while the Pre-Raphaelites held a well-deserved grudge against Dickens (whose attack on them had aroused strong public support for him – and antagonism for the PRB), until Harriet Collins, the mother of Wilkie and Charlie, intervened. She knew both Charles Dickens and John Everett Millais well and felt that if they met properly, they would like each other; so she arranged a party and invited them. As Katey Dickens would later reveal, Dickens was embarrassed by the widespread adverse repercussions that 'Old Lamps for New Ones' had inflicted on so many artists and prepared to extend the hand of friendship to Millais, whose work he had grown to admire. This photograph of Millais (opposite) was taken in 1857, as part of a series for a photographic gallery of celebrities. Millais wrote that it was 'considered by all an admirable likeness'. Three years later, in 1860, Katey would model for what proved one of Millais's most popular paintings, The Black Brunswicker.

William Holman Hunt (1827–1910)

The best man at Katey and Charlie's wedding was the Pre-Raphaelite artist William Holman Hunt. He had still not entirely forgiven Dickens for his scathing review of his and Millais's paintings nine years earlier. At the wedding breakfast he sat next to Dickens and recorded that the father of the bride was in a bad mood: annoyed and argumentative, and unnecessarily heated during a discussion about art. By this date, Holman Hunt had begun to make a name for himself. He would go on to become one of the most highly respected, and highly paid, artists in Britain. Despite having been the most conventional of the Pre-Raphaelite Brothers, he was unable to avoid scandal. In 1865, having ended an unsuitable engagement to the Pre-Raphaelite model Annie Miller, Holman Hunt made a good marriage to a woman named Fanny Waugh, who was thirty-two years old and had been expected to remain single. Holman Hunt was a regular visitor to the Middle East, where he adored the light and was inspired by the people, history and landscapes. While travelling to the Middle East via Italy, Fanny gave birth to their son, Cyril. She died a few weeks later, just before their first wedding anniversary. Nine years later, Holman Hunt realised he had fallen in love with Fanny's younger sister, Edith, who had been helping to care for Cyril – but it was illegal in Britain to marry a deceased wife's sister. The couple married in Italy, and Holman Hunt spent years attempting to change the law to permit widowers to marry their sisters-in-law.

....
OPPOSITE
William Holman Hunt
Elliott & Fry, 1865

Henry Chorley (1808–72)

Throughout the 1850s, the critic and writer Henry Chorley was a constant visitor both to Tavistock House and to Gad's Hill Place, the house in Kent that Dickens bought in 1856. Chorley was born in Lancashire, where he began his career as an office clerk, but like the young Dickens he had dreams of a more literary future, so he moved to London in 1833 to work for *The Athenaeum* magazine. There he wrote literary reviews and articles about music. He also attempted to make his name as a dramatist, although his plays received little acclaim. Chorley was friends with many of the most famous writers of the age, including Robert Browning and Elizabeth Barrett Browning. His name crops up several times in Elizabeth's correspondence, often in letters to their mutual friend Mary Russell Mitford. One of Mitford's letters to Elizabeth shows great displeasure with Chorley, and she refers to him as a 'presumptuous coxcomb'. It seems she was offended by his choice of brightly coloured waistcoats – a fashion for which Dickens was also alternately admired and derided, with critics accusing him of being 'vulgar' at a time when most men wore sombre colours. Dickens, however, like Chorley, had grown up in the age of the Prince Regent, when men's fashion was much more interesting and flamboyant than it had become by the mid-Victorian age.

....
OPPOSITE
The Dickens family and friends in the porch at Gad's Hill Place, Kent
Robert Hindry Mason for Mason & Co., 1865
Standing (left to right): Henry Fothergill Chorley, Katey Collins
(née Dickens), Mamie Dickens and Charles Dickens
Seated: Charles Allston Collins and Georgina Hogarth

Gad's Hill Place, Kent
From the *Illustrated London News*, 18 June 1870
Situated between Higham and Rochester, this fine house
was Charles Dickens's country home from June 1857
(although he bought it over a year earlier).

It became apparent that there was another attraction to
the Dickens household for Chorley, aside from his friendship
with Charles: he was unrequitedly in love with Mamie Dickens,
who was thirty years his junior. After his death, Mamie would
discover that he had bequeathed her a lifetime annuity.

There is a touching story associated with Gad's Hill Place. When Dickens was a young child living in Kent with his family, he and his father would go walking together. They often passed a large house, and John Dickens would point it out to his son, telling him that if he worked hard and made a lot of money when he grew up, one day he would be able to buy it. For the young Dickens that house remained a magical place, and when he happened to hear, by chance, in the mid-1850s that it was up for sale, he bought it. Gad's Hill Place, located on the road between Higham and Rochester, was the only home that Dickens ever owned – all his London homes were rented on long leases (as was usual at the time). Being able to buy a country home with land and privacy was, for Dickens, a way of laying to rest, at last, the ghost of his childhood; he was proud, too, that Gad's Hill itself was mentioned by Shakespeare in his Henriad trilogy. Dickens's return to Kent took him back to the place where he had been happiest, and he spent as much time at Gad's Hill as possible.

Throughout his final years in London and Kent, Dickens's output was unceasing. He wrote *Hard Times*, *Little Dorrit*, *A Tale of Two Cities*, *Great Expectations*, *Our Mutual Friend* and, although unfinished, *The Mystery of Edwin Drood*. He also turned out numerous magazine articles and short stories, as well as two books for children: *A Child's History of England* and *The Life of Our Lord* (written for his own family).

Dickens in the study at Gad's Hill Place, Kent
S. Hollyer. Published *c*.1875
Behind Dickens can be seen a door made out of a false bookcase, which he brought with him from Tavistock House. The fake books' titles include *Cat's Lives* (in nine volumes) and *Hansard's Guide to Refreshing Sleep*.

Edward Bulwer-Lytton (1803–73)

The writer and politician Edward Bulwer-Lytton was a welcome addition to Dickens's circle at this time. The two men had met in the 1830s, from when this portrait dates, but their friendship grew closer in the late 1840s. In 1852, Charles and Catherine named their youngest child after him: Edward Bulwer-Lytton Dickens (known as 'Plorn'). In 1850, Bulwer-Lytton had been in the cast of Dickens's amateur-theatrical performances of *Every Man in his Humour* by Ben Jonson. It was then that he

Edward Bulwer-Lytton, 1st Baron Lytton
Henry William Pickersgill, c.1831

had the idea of starting a fund to help artists and writers in financial need. His friends loved the idea, and the fund became known as The Guild of Literature and Art. Dickens and Augustus Egg were also influential in its creation, with Dickens playing an active part in its administration for several years before becoming disillusioned by too much bureaucracy. The Guild outlived all its founders, remaining in existence until 1897.

Perhaps one of the reasons that the friendship between Bulwer-Lytton and Dickens grew stronger in the 1850s was the deterioration in the Dickenses' marriage. While Dickens was growing restless, he was aware that Bulwer-Lytton had been through a scandalous separation more than a decade earlier. After an embittered, increasingly public battle, Bulwer-Lytton had his wife Rosina declared insane and incarcerated in an asylum. At a time when men held legal power over their wives, few women could withstand such treatment, but Rosina Bulwer-Lytton convinced the asylum medical staff that she was sane. She was released after three weeks, after which she continued to rail against her husband, even more publicly. While Bulwer-Lytton tried to shore up his position as a pillar of society, his estranged wife denounced him as a liar and a hypocrite; she even published a book in which she lampooned him. It was ostensibly a novel, but few people believed it was a work of fiction.

Despite the scandal, Bulwer-Lytton remained a popular writer. His works include *Pelham, or the Adventures of a Gentleman* (1828), *The Caxtons* (1849), *The Last Days of Pompeii* (1834) and *Paul Clifford* (1830), the latter opening with the now-famous cliché: 'It was a dark and stormy night'. Perhaps as Dickens began to feel trapped within his own marriage, he empathised more with Bulwer-Lytton, seeing him as an ally for what he felt lay ahead.

Hans Christian Andersen (1805–75)

One of the people who came to stay at Gad's Hill Place around this time was the Danish writer Hans Christian Andersen. Dickens and Andersen first met, in 1847, while Andersen was touring England, at the London salon of the Irish writer and society hostess Marguerite, Countess of Blessington. The two men corresponded for a decade, and, in 1857, Andersen was invited to stay for a few days; he then outstayed his welcome by several weeks. Andersen's letters to the Danish queen during his sojourn in Kent suggest that he had no idea how unwelcome he was becoming as his visit stretched on. One of the reasons the Dickens children grew to resent him was Andersen's insistence that, in Denmark, it was customary for male guests to be shaved every day by one of the sons of the house. Dickens made Andersen a daily appointment with a local barber. The children were also astounded when Andersen lay on the lawn and sobbed like a child, after receiving in the post an unfavourable review of one of his books. By the end of Andersen's five weeks in Kent, the friendship had soured. Dickens and Andersen never regained their former easy correspondence.

By the late 1850s, Dickens had begun to fall out with many of his former friends and acquaintances. Perhaps one of the reasons that he cooled towards Andersen was not only because he stayed too long but also because Andersen published in a German newspaper an article about his time in the Dickens household, which noted especially how lovely Catherine Dickens

············
OPPOSITE
Hans Christian Andersen
Hansen, Schou & Weller, 1869

had been to him. This was at a time when Dickens wanted the public to see him, not Catherine, in a positive light.

For some years, Catherine had been aware that Charles had fallen out of love with her; by 1858, she knew she had lost her fight to keep her husband and was devastated by the impending legal separation. Society drawing rooms became filled with whispered scandal about the end of the Dickens marriage. As Dickens tried to keep his reputation intact, his fans whispered horrible rumours about Catherine; stories contended she was an alcoholic and that her children had never loved her. When Catherine was sent away to live in Regent's Park, Dickens kept all the children with him, the law stating that children were the legal property of the father. Charley, however, insisted on living with his mother, but the other Dickens children were given no choice, despite being divided in their loyalties.

Although Dickens claimed in an article written about the end of his marriage that he and Catherine had become incompatible – that the separation was amicable – few people were fooled by this. Elizabeth Barrett Browning echoed the feelings of many women of the time when she wrote in a letter:

What is this sad story about Dickens and his wife? Incompatibility of temper after twenty-three years of married life? What a plea! ... Poor woman! She must suffer bitterly – that is sure.

It was while his marriage was coming to a painful end that Dickens launched a new career. Alongside his writing, he began composing public readings of his works. This satisfied both the actor and the author within him; as soon as he set out on his

Charles Dickens
Harry Furniss, date uncertain, 1880–1910
Furniss's cartoon was inspired by reports that Dickens had worn himself out with his intensely emotional readings of Nancy's murder from *Oliver Twist* (the scene appears on the wall behind him).

reading tours, the public was enthralled. He travelled the country, performing to sell-out audiences. His friends and family, worried about his health, became concerned by the passion and fury with which he read certain scenes, particularly his favourite reading, the passage where Bill Sikes murders Nancy from *Oliver Twist*, during which he became very angry and red-faced. Dickens undertook extensive reading tours from 1858 until early 1870, when he was persuaded to stop for the sake of his health.

Ellen Ternan (1839–1914)

The overriding reason that had persuaded Dickens to
end his troubled marriage was because he had fallen in love
with another woman: Ellen Ternan. The problems within his
marriage had come to a head in 1857, during a production of
The Frozen Deep. The cast had performed the play in London, with
the usual group of family and friends, but when it came to going
on tour, they needed to hire professionals for the female roles.
A theatrical friend suggested a family of actresses: the widowed
Mrs Ternan and her three daughters. Dickens fell in love with
the youngest, Ellen, who was eighteen, a year younger than
Mamie Dickens and the same age as Katey; he was forty-five.

Ellen Ternan stayed in a relationship with Dickens until
his death in 1870, after which she and her family colluded in
turning back the clock. Somehow Ellen had to account for all
the years of being Dickens's mistress, and the easiest way to do
it was to make the still youthful-looking actress play the role of
a much younger woman. She went from being thirty-two years
old to telling people she was eighteen. Astoundingly, she
managed it and then went on to marry a schoolteacher, who was
also a church minister, and have two children. What her husband
presumably never knew was that she had also had a child with
Charles Dickens. The existence of a Dickens-Ternan baby is
disputed, but Katey Dickens admitted to a friend towards the end
of her life that Ellen had given birth to a baby boy, who had died.
Marie Dickens, the widow of Henry Fielding Dickens (the only

one of the Dickens children to go to university and who went on to become a prominent barrister), also confirmed this. Ellen's story has remained that of a woman in the shadows. Most poignantly, after thirteen years with Dickens she was 'written out' even at his death. The official records show that fourteen people attended Charles Dickens's private funeral at London's Westminster Abbey; yet the Abbey's archives record only thirteen names. Ellen's is not among them.

There is a strange coincidence associated with Ellen Ternan, who survived her much older lover by many years. Following her death in 1914, Ellen was buried at Highland Road Cemetery in Southsea, just outside Portsmouth (the widowed Ellen had been living in Southsea with her sister). Not only is this cemetery a short distance from the house where Dickens was born but also, in the very same cemetery, is buried another woman with whom he had been in love: Maria Winter (née Beadnell), Dickens's first love, the young woman who broke his heart when he was a teenager.

....

Dickens himself is buried at Poets' Corner, the section of Westminster Abbey reserved for writers. After the small, private funeral, the grave was left open for two days, so that mourners could pay their respects. Thousands of people travelled from all over England to say goodbye to Boz. Henry Fielding Dickens was told by a friend that he had been in a tobacconist's when he heard the news of Henry's father's death. He said that a working man had entered the shop and announced: 'Charles Dickens is dead. We have lost our best friend.'

SELECT BIBLIOGRAPHY

Peter Ackroyd, *Dickens* (Random House, London, 2002)

Rosemarie Bodenheimer, *Knowing Dickens* (Cornell University Press, Ithaca NY, 2010)

Caroline Dakers, *The Holland Park Circle* (Yale University Press, London & New Haven CT, 1999)

Lucinda Dickens Hawksley, *Charles Dickens* (Carlton Books, London, 2011)

John Forster, *The Life of Charles Dickens* (Tebbo, Queensland [Australia], 2012)

Lucinda Hawksley, *Katey, The Life and Loves of Dickens's Artist Daughter* (Doubleday, London, 2006)

Edgar Johnson, *Charles Dickens, His Tragedy and Triumph* (Simon & Schuster, New York, 1952)

Andrew Lycett, *Wilkie Collins: A Life of Sensation* (Hutchinson, London, 2013)

Lilian Nayder, *The Other Dickens: A Life of Catherine Hogarth* (Cornell University Press, Ithaca NY, 2012)

Michael Slater, *Charles Dickens* (Yale University Press, London & New Haven CT, 2009)

— *The Great Charles Dickens Scandal* (Yale University Press, London & New Haven CT, 2014)

Claire Tomalin, *The Invisible Woman: The Story of Nelly Ternan and Charles Dickens* (Penguin, London, 1990)

— *Charles Dickens: A Life* (Penguin, London, 2012)

MAJOR WORKS OF CHARLES DICKENS

Charles Dickens, *Sketches by Boz* (London, 1836)
— *The Pickwick Papers* (London, 1836–7)
— *The Mudfog Papers* (London, 1838)
— *Oliver Twist* (London, 1837–9)
— *Nicholas Nickleby* (London, 1838–9)
— *The Old Curiosity Shop* (London, 1840–1)
— *Barnaby Rudge* (London, 1841)
— *American Notes* (London, 1842)
— *Martin Chuzzlewit* (London, 1843–4)
— *A Christmas Carol* (London, 1843)
— *The Chimes* (London, 1844)
— *The Cricket on the Hearth* (London, 1845)
— *The Battle of Life* (London, 1846)
— *Pictures from Italy* (London, 1846)
— *Dombey and Son* (London, 1846–8)
— *The Life of our Lord* (London, 1846–9)
— *The Haunted Man* (London, 1848)
— *David Copperfield* (London, 1848–50)
— *Bleak House* (London, 1851–3)
— *A Child's History of England* (London, 1851–3)
— *Hard Times* (London, 1854)
— *Little Dorrit* (London, 1855–7)
— *A Tale of Two Cities* (London, 1859)
— *Great Expectations* (London, 1861)
— *Our Mutual Friend* (London, 1864–5)
— *The Mystery of Edwin Drood* (London, 1870)

LIST OF ILLUSTRATIONS

Albumen carte-de-visite, 92 x 59mm.
© National Portrait Gallery, London
(NPG Ax28966)
p.99 The Dickens family and friends in the
porch at Gad's Hill Place, Kent, Robert
Hindry Mason for Mason & Co., 1865.
Reproduced by courtesy of Charles
Dickens Museum, London
p.100 Gad's Hill Place, Kent, unknown artist.
Published in the *Illustrated London News*, 18
June 1870. www.victorianpicturelibrary.com
pp.102–3 Dickens in the study at Gad's Hill
Place, Kent, S. Hollyer. Published c.1875.
Library of Congress, Prints & Photographs
Division, LC-DIG-pga-07120
p.104 Edward Bulwer-Lytton, 1st Baron Lytton,
Henry William Pickersgill, c.1831. Oil on
canvas, 914 x 715mm. © National Portrait
Gallery, London (NPG 1277)
p.106 Hans Christian Andersen, Hansen, Schou
& Weller, 1869. Albumen carte-de-visite,
88 x 57mm. © National Portrait Gallery,
London (NPG x5791)
p.109 Charles Dickens, Harry Furniss,
date uncertain, 1880–1910. Pen and ink,
270 x 248mm. © National Portrait Gallery,
London (NPG 3566)
p.110 Ellen Ternan, unknown photographer,
n.d. Reproduced by courtesy of Charles
Dickens Museum, London
p.120 Charles Dickens, John & Charles
Watkins, 1863. Albumen print on card,
203 x 163mm. © National Portrait Gallery,
London (NPG x14339)

ACKNOWLEDGEMENTS

With thanks to Christopher Tinker,
Nicola Saunders, Kathleen Bloomfield,
Ruth Müller-Wirth and Hattie Clarke at
National Portrait Gallery Publications,
copy-editor Helen Armitage, proofreader
Denny Hemming, indexer Lisa Footitt,
designers Emma and Alex Smith at Smith
& Gilmour, my agent Broo Doherty at
DHH and Louisa Price at the Charles
Dickens Museum.

INDEX

Note: page numbers in **bold** refer to captions.